FAIR IS OUR LAND

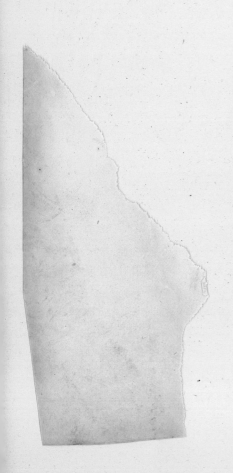

BRUTON PARISH CHURCH—Williamsburg, Virginia

Pen Drawing by Samuel Chamberlain

FAIR IS OUR LAND

Designed and Edited by
SAMUEL CHAMBERLAIN
Introduction by DONALD MOFFAT

HASTINGS HOUSE, *Publishers*   NEW YORK CITY

PUBLISHED, JULY 30, 1942

SECOND PRINTING, AUGUST 17, 1942

THIRD PRINTING, MARCH 10, 1943

FOURTH PRINTING, MARCH 9, 1944

FIFTH PRINTING, DECEMBER 5, 1944

SIXTH PRINTING, FEBRUARY 20, 1946

SEVENTH PRINTING, JUNE 14, 1946

O I see flashing that this America is only you and me,
Its power, weapons, testimony, are you and me,
Its crimes, lies, thefts, defections, are you and me . . .
Freedom, language, poems, employments, are you and me,
Past, present, future, are you and me . . .

I am for those that have never been master'd,
For men and women whose tempers have never been master'd
For those whom laws, theories, conventions, can never master.
I am for those who walk abreast with the whole earth,
Who inaugurate one to inaugurate all . . .

(Democracy, while weapons were everywhere aim'd at your breast,
I saw you serenely giving birth to immortal children, saw in dreams
  your dilating form,
Saw you with spreading mantle covering the world.)

WALT WHITMAN: *By Blue Ontario's Shores*

A BUCKS COUNTY FARMHOUSE   *Wood Engraving by Thomas W. Nason*

Introduction

I HAPPENED to be picking raspberries when I heard that the war was over. Berries won't wait; I went on picking—fingers occupied and mind free to ponder.

The best berries, like the best of most things, grow hidden away out of sight. You have to bend double to find them, peering up through the forest of brown canes and pale green shoots and yellowing leaves to where they dangle, protected from wind and sun, on filaments almost too fine to bear their weight. They hang in jeweled clusters, purple in the shade, translucent crimson where a sunbeam catches them.

At the end of the first row, my quart measure nearly filled, I stood up to ease my back, and looked out. I saw the sloping meadow beside the raspberry patch; beside it, the stand of spruce and fir in a hundred different shades of green; and beyond, a glimpse of blue water, stained silver by the shining tide-slick, and the purple hills of the distant mainland out across the bay. Standing thus at the very edge of America, sweat on my back and the sun pouring down, behind me the white clapboard farmhouse, the woodpile, the apple trees and lilacs, and the junipered gray ledges cropping out of the bit of lawn, my eyes went on and on; I saw the country whole, and suddenly I *knew* that the war had not been fought in vain. There it lay under my mind's eye, our ancient heritage; and I prayed that we might have the wisdom, faith, and courage to be worthy of it in peace as we had been in war.

We are Americans. Yet, standing in the sun that day, it came to me that we had won the war not because we are Americans, but because we are free men; and the reason we are free is that we have never been content with anything less. Our land was conceived in freedom. Our settlements were struck from the wilderness by men and women who by sheer instinct set themselves to searching out new places in the land where they could live in freedom. They carried the seed to the outermost limits of the continent and beyond, and planted it, and tended it while it grew, and reaped its fruits. And when we built our great cities a handful of it went into every cornerstone.

Always we have had to defend it against the attacks of enemies, both foreign and domestic. Only once have we taken up arms against each other. We have learned a better way: laughter, child of common sense. Whenever some incipient tyrant has appeared and begun to grow too big for his boots, whenever some stupid statute has been enacted while we looked the other way, we have simply ignored them both, by a sort of mass consensus, and gone our way. Laughter is a weapon feared by tyranny above all others.

There is no stick long enough to measure the depth of our dis-

WOODED SHORE—Maine   *Wood Engraving by Thomas W. Nason*

taste for war. Yet our late enemies, once they missed overwhelming the free nations at the first onslaught, never had a chance of winning. Perhaps they are not to blame for failing to understand. There was nothing in their traditions to teach them that mere military virtuosity, the product of years of close and careful discipline, is the hotbed not of victory but of defeat. How could they know that free men cannot, in the long run, ever be beaten? Once again we have proved that the so-called art of war is *not* mysterious, *not* glorious, *not* even an art. Free men can master all the tricks overnight. Let us hope that our enemies have learned their lesson, as we have learned once more what a shabby business war is, how childish its traditional pomp and trappings, as it has ever been, from the days of the spear and crossbow to the modern era of total destruction.

Now from every corner of the world free men in uniform have been filtering home by the million, each to the beloved acre whose image he has carried in his heart over a thousand leagues of land and sea. Americans had turned fighting men for a time, on compulsion; but never for an instant had they thought of giving up their membership in the company of free civilians. Civilians they were born, as civilians again they will die.

Unchanged? Not quite. Americans have looked into the four corners of the world. For the first time most of us have left the fireside, learned from the evidence of our very eyes how other people live, seen the beauty and variety of the lands they dwell in; and know now, by firsthand experience, that to no other people in the world has nature been more generous in her gifts. The fighting free man, home again, knows now what he was fighting for, and knows it was worth the fight.

At no time in history have so many American men and women been compelled to leave their homes and move from place to place, within the United States and beyond its shores. At no time have so many of us been given the opportunity to see and compare. Nine young Americans out of ten have been sent, if not abroad, at least to hitherto unfamiliar parts of his own country, and learned, incidentally, that the people who live in them, barring local accent and custom, look a whole lot like the folks back home.

To those who served their country in foreign lands, patriotism has taken on new meaning, based not on sheer native pride but on observation. We had understood, in a vague sort of way, and unconsciously accepted, the thing called liberty; but we had little idea, till we saw the effects of bondage on other countries, what freedom really meant. Bondage may be of many kinds other than mere economic serfdom. It may be rooted in ignorance, superstition, custom, tradition; the mere habit of wearing chains may make the wearers unhappy without them. In many countries the very fact that a certain thing has always been done in a certain way—drawing water, for example, or planting corn, or carrying burdens, or pray-

WINDSWEPT   *Wood Engraving by Thomas W. Nason*

ing—is reason enough to go on doing it that way. (It is an American trait, and one of the hallmarks of the free man, never to be satisfied with the way grandfather did it, but to set about finding a better, quicker method.) Traditional emperor-worship in Japan, traditional caste-worship in Germany, are forces much more binding on the people of each country than any statutory law could be. Because our government derives its authority from our very selves, we are happily free from such tabus and traditions. We have heard it said over and over again from kindergarten on. But now we have seen for ourselves. Now we know.

Americans have a reputation for boastfulness. I wonder. Serving aboard a small Navy vessel during the late unpleasantness gave me, for the first time, a chance to get acquainted with men from every part of the country. In age they ranged from seventeen to sixty, in color from coal black through yellow and brown to white. Every native stock of the northern hemisphere was represented among the crew of my ship at one time or another: English, Irish, Scottish, Welsh, French, Portuguese, German, Italian, Swedish, Norwegian, Polish, Greek, all the Baltic and Balkan states—not a race was missing. There were Jews, Catholics, Protestants of every denomination, Russian and Greek Orthodox, and other beliefs I had never heard of; there were those who read their racing forms and others who read their Bibles; most of them were good men and a few were not good and one or two were evil. They all had this in common: they were Americans. They couldn't possibly be mistaken for anything else, and they were proud of it.

Well, what did we talk about? The flag? Our glorious Navy? My country, right or wrong? Never a word. Maybe we took them for granted, or maybe such sentiments lie too deep for words. We talked girls and food and drink and sport and money and after-the-war, of course. And, sure enough, we boasted. But not about the United States. When we started chucking our weight around it was always first about our own section of the country—North, South, East, or West—with pity for the poor devils who had the bad luck to be born in any of the other three. Next we boasted of our home State; and then of our own particular bit of it—our home town, city, suburb, farm, hillside, seacoast, or river valley. And when we really hit our stride the subject was not, as you might expect, the wealth and progressiveness of our home town, but how pretty it is back there. Never a moment that we weren't homesick for remembered beauty, though not all of us said so with flowers.

There are places in the world, no doubt, as fair as anything in America. But is there—I wonder—anywhere a piece of it that can show beauty in such infinite variety. There is nothing in the East like the Yosemite, to be sure; but then, there is nothing in the West to touch the modest loveliness of an upland farm in Vermont. Noth-

14   FAIR IS OUR LAND

COUNTRY ROAD   *Wood Engraving by Thomas W. Nason*

ing in the South is remotely comparable to the Dakota prairies, and the North can show nothing like the ancient live oaks of our Southeastern States. No wonder our pride tends to be local. But now the Yankee farm boy has seen the wonder of California's giant sequoias, the Idaho rancher has hunted submarines in the Gulf of Maine, Brooklyn has visited the Painted Desert, Mississippi has bootcamped on the shore of Lake Michigan, the Kentucky mountaineer has walked the sidewalks of New York and San Francisco. Not one of them will admit for an instant that any other part of the country can hold a candle to his own piece of it—I happen to know, for instance, that the world's prettiest spot is a certain rocky cove on a certain little island off the coast of Maine. But now millions of us have had a chance to see the country as a whole, and have come to understand the grandeur of its scale and scope, the undefiled purity of its mountains and deserts and plains, the friendly simplicity of the little places where men have made their homes.

We know now that this country of ours is worth cherishing, serving, worthy of our faith in it. The pictures in this book show the grandeur and beauty of our land. In many of them you will see a man's figure—no legendary Paul Bunyan, Pecos Bill, or John Henry, but a simple American. A shepherd leans on his stick, the prairie sweeping away before him; a roadside storekeeper peddles the great American staples, five gallons of gas and a hot-dog; a tourist sits on a log in the shade of a mighty stand of Douglas firs; here a New Hampshire farmhand sweats over the haying on his sun-drenched hillside farm, and here a mountaineer rests on the rooftree of the world to swing his eye over the savage white convulsion of the Rocky Mountains. Wherever you find him, you, a stranger, will find him simple, original, friendly and, if you don't make a fool of yourself, ready to do you a favor. He can afford to be hospitable: he is a free man, therefore unafraid. He is his own master: where he pitches his shack he's the boss, and you, the stranger passing through, are his friend.

Today, he is the most powerful man in the world. Also, he is having a serious love affair with his country. It is a combination that augurs well for the world, if he keeps his head. For there are two kinds of patriotism. One of them leads to war. The day is fast approaching—indeed it is already here, if we have the wisdom to perceive it—when this kind of patriotism will prove a luxury we cannot afford, if life is to survive on the planet.

But there is a deeper, more generous form of patriotism. It has nothing to do with national ambition, with the covetousness whose other name is imperialism. Another name for it is self-respect, the simple self-respect of free men. Like other kinds of love, it finds its nourishment in the still places of the soul, in the hidden chambers of the heart. It is rooted in strength. It can afford to be generous to the weak, patient with the strong.

We are seeing again the matchless beauty of our own beloved country in the clear new radiance that courage and sacrifice have lighted in our hearts. Let us in all humility learn to be worthy of this shining land of ours.

DONALD MOFFAT

MASSACHUSETTS HALL, HARVARD
Wood Engraving by Thomas W. Nason

Contents

BERKSHIRE HILLS   *Wood Engraving by Thomas W. Nason*

Editor's Note

THIS VOLUME seeks to portray the beauty of the American countryside. It does not encompass the might of our cities nor the dynamic energy of our industry. That is a theme for a book in itself. Above all, it is not a state-by-state encyclopedia of scenic wonders. Its objective is to distill the essence of rural America. The work of more than eighty etchers and photographers has been selected to give an unforgettable *impression* of this bright land. Their eloquent pictures speak for themselves, without the need of an interlocutor.

Many schools of thought are represented by these eighty artists. Among the etchers are both moderns and conservatives. The photographers are widely diversified. There are abstractionists, pictorialists, salon exhibitors and architectural specialists among them. Each makes a distinct contribution to the composite portrait of our homeland. To each I beg to express the keenest thanks and appreciation. I am grateful to the Library of Congress, the New York Public Library, Kennedy & Company, New York, and Goodspeed's Book Shop, Boston, for supplying the etchings for these reproductions. Finally, may I pay particular tribute to the assistance offered by the Farm Security Administration, the United States Forest Service and the United States Department of the Interior, all in Washington.

Here, then, is *your* America, a matchlessly fair land and a brave one.

SAMUEL CHAMBERLAIN

BLACKSMITH'S SHOP   *Thomas W. Nason*

FAIR IS OUR LAND

Pownal, Vermont   *Gustav Anderson*

Towns and Villages

Midwinter – West Hartford, Vermont   *Marion Post Wolcott for F.S.A.*

Wooden Gothic – Lancaster, New Hampshire   *Rothstein for F.S.A.*

FAIR IS OUR LAND

The Frary House – Old Deerfield, Massachusetts   *Samuel Chamberlain*

Berkshire Night   *Etching by Kerr Eby*

TOWNS AND VILLAGES

Summer Street

Drypoint by Samuel Chamberlain

FAIR IS OUR LAND

Bend in the Road – Newcastle, New Hampshire   *Drypoint by Samuel Chamberlain*

Springtime in the Village – Peterburg, New York   *Keystone*

TOWNS AND VILLAGES

Northernmost New England – Fort Kent, Maine   *Delano for F.S.A.*

New England Night   *Lithograph by C. W. Anderson*

FAIR IS OUR LAND

Cornwall Bridge   *Etching by Armin Landeck*

Easthampton, Long Island   *Tet Borsig*

TOWNS AND VILLAGES   31

Porch Light – Pierre, South Dakota   *Vachon for F.S.A.*

Main Street – Grundy Center, Iowa   *Rothstein for F.S.A.*

Mrs. Ellis' Store – Falmouth, Virginia   *Frances Benjamin Johnston*

Prairie Village – Surrey, North Dakota *Vachon for F.S.A.*

Tank Town – Bridgeport, Wisconsin *Vachon for F.S.A.*

34

FAIR IS OUR LAND

Colorado Hill Town – Ouray   *Rothstein for F.S.A.*

TOWNS AND VILLAGES

Ghost Town – Eureka, Colorado   *Lee for F.S.A.*

Silverton, Colorado   *Lee for F.S.A.*

FAIR IS OUR LAND

Silver Peak, Nevada   *Rothstein for F.S.A.*

Pre-historic Village – Mesa Verde   *Cedric Wright*

Montana Prairie Town   *Rothstein for F.S.A.*

Pueblo Village – Taos, New Mexico   *Rothstein for F.S.A.*

FAIR IS OUR LAND

Hinckley Lake – Ohio

Ewing Galloway

Inland Waters

Lake in the Hills – North Carolina

FAIR IS OUR LAND

Sunset on Newfound Lake – New Hampshire *Arthur Hammond*

Sand Dunes on Lake Michigan *Underwood and Underwood*

INLAND WATERS

Trapper's Lake – Colorado   *U. S. Forest Service*

Lake Tarryall   *Lithograph by Adolph Dehn*

Tilden Lake – Yosemite National Park

Cedric Wright

Klamath Lake – Oregon   *Ray Atkeson*

Spirit Lake and Mt. St. Helens   *Ray Atkeson*

Gold Mill – Colorado   *Lee for F.S.A.*

San Carlos Lake – Arizona   *Josef Muench*

St. Mary's Lake – Glacier National Park *U. S. Dept. of the Interior*

Seven Lakes Basin – Olympic National Park *Asahel Curtis for U. S. Dept. of the Int.*

Crater Lake – Oregon   *Ray Atkeson*

Lost Lake – Oregon   *Ray Atkeson*

Trick Falls – Glacier National Park

Hileman

FAIR IS OUR LAND

Niagara Falls   *Ewing Galloway*

The Dam at Pigeon Forge – Tennessee   *Ewing Galloway*

INLAND WATERS

Punch Bowl Falls – Oregon

C. M. Ballard for U. S. Forest Service

Swift Current Falls – Montana

Hileman for Glacier National Park

FAIR IS OUR LAND

Glen Aulin Falls – California   *Cedric Wright*

River Bend in Provo Canyon – Utah   *Ray Atkeson*

INLAND WATERS   51

The York River – Maine   *Etching by R. Stephens Wright*

Curiosity   *Etching by Frank Besedick*

The Sweeping Ohio   *B. W. Muir for U. S. Forest Service*

Steamboat on the Kentucky River   *Ewing Galloway*

INLAND WATERS   53

West Point   *Etching by Gerald K. Geerlings*

Mississippi Evening   *Etching by Otto Kuhler*

The Amy Hewes – Louisiana *Ewing Galloway*

Mississippi River Ferry – Helena, Arkansas *Arkansas State Publicity Department*

INLAND WATERS

The Colorado River   *Hubert A. Lowman*

North Platte River – Nebraska   *Underwood and Underwood*

FAIR IS OUR LAND

High Water on the Sacramento River

Grant Duggins

INLAND WATERS

The Columbia River Gorge   *Ray Atkeson*

Indian Salmon Fishermen – Columbia River   *Ray Atkeson*

FAIR IS OUR LAND

The Grande Ronde Valley – Oregon   *Minor White*

The Farm

A Pennsylvania Landscape   *Woodcut by Thomas Nason*

Farm on the River   *Drypoint by Chauncey E. Ryder*

FAIR IS OUR LAND

August Afternoon on the Farm – Rowley, Massachusetts   *Samuel Chamberlain*

Hilltop   *Eleanor Park Custis*

THE FARM   61

Barns in Winter – Putney, Vermont   *Marion Post Wolcott for F.S.A.*

The Casey Farm – North Kingston, Rhode Island   *Samuel Chamberlain*

FAIR IS OUR LAND

Abandoned Farm – Hampton Falls, New Hampshire   *Samuel Chamberlain*

Hay Cutting Time in Vermont   *Rothstein for the F.S.A.*

THE FARM

New England Farm on the Merrimac

Eleanor Park Custis

FAIR IS OUR LAND

Pennsylvania Farmland   *Marion Post Wolcott for F.S.A.*

Harvest in Ohio   *Ewing Galloway*

Farm on the Atlantic Shore   *Samuel Chamberlain*

Barns of Purissima   *C. Stanton Loeber*

String Bean Pickers – Cambridge, Maryland *Rothstein for F.S.A.*

Barn With Stone Silos – Maryland *Henry Flannery*

Log Farm House – Roanoke, Virginia   *Frances Benjamin Johnston*

Old Slave Quarters – Eastville, Virginia   *Frances Benjamin Johnston*

FAIR IS OUR LAND

Upland Farms of Virginia – Autumn Near Marion.   *Marion Wolcott for F.S.A.*

Upland Farms of Virginia – Winter – Rappahannock County *Rothstein for F.S.A.*

THE FARM   69

Tobacco Field in the Kentucky Mountains   *Marion Post Wolcott for F.S.A.*

Tobacco Harvest   *Marion Post Wolcott for F.S.A.*

Contrasting Farms in Kentucky – The Backwoods   *Marion Post Wolcott for F.S.A.*

Dairy Farm in Jefferson County – Kentucky   *Marion Post Wolcott for F.S.A.*

THE FARM

Mississippi Mule Team   *Marion Post Wolcott for F.S.A.*

Cotton Picking Time – Benoit, Mississippi   *Marion Post Wolcott for F.S.A.*

The Fertile Earth   *Lithograph by Albert W. Barker*

THE FARM

Footbridge – Ohio
Rothstein for F.S.A.

Wisconsin Silo
Vories Fisher

FAIR IS OUR LAND

Pumpkin Pattern   *Ewing Galloway*

Harvest in Pennsylvania   *Delano for F.S.A.*

March Winds   *J. H. Thomas*

Feeding Time – Iowa   *Rothstein for F.S.A.*

Kansas Corn   *Keystone*

THE FARM

Cloudy Sky   *Etching by John E. Costigan*

Early Planting   *Etching by Kerr Eby*

Sunset – Imperial, Nebraska   *Rothstein for F.S.A.*

Nebraska Loam   *Rothstein for F.S.A.*

THE FARM

Colorado Foothills   *Lee for F.S.A.*

The Thresher – Utah   *Lee for F.S.A.*

FAIR IS OUR LAND

Split Rail Fence – Muncie, Indiana

Ewing Galloway

Farm Pattern in Iowa

Rothstein for F.S.A.

THE FARM

Sheep Ranch in Oregon   *Rothstein for F.S.A.*

Oregon Pastorale   *Ray Atkeson*

Sixteen Horse Combine – Eastern Washington   *Rothstein for F.S.A.*

The Palouse Wheat Country – Washington   *Rothstein for F.S.A.*

THE FARM

Lettuce Factory – Salinas, California   *Orville Logan*

North Powder Valley Farm – Oregon   *Minor White*

Paysage   *Pierson Studio*

The Countryside

IN THE EAST AND SOUTH

Village in the Hills – East Corinth, Vermont   *Ewing Galloway*

Salt Marshes   *Etching by Kerr Eby*

The Gladstone Road – Winter

Thomas O. Sheckell

Saunderstown Fields

Drypoint by Samuel Chamberlain

THE COUNTRYSIDE

Winter Shadows – Stowe, Vermont   *Marion Post Wolcott for F.S.A.*

Haying Time in Vermont   *Tet Borsig*

New England Winter – Essex, Massachusetts   *Samuel Chamberlain*

Sunlit Forest   *Lithograph by Stow Wengenroth*

THE COUNTRYSIDE

Maples in Early Spring

Etching by Childe Hassam

FAIR IS OUR LAND

Cider Mill   *Etching by Kerr Eby*

The Old Farm   *Etching by C. W. Anderson*

Covered Bridge   *Frank R. Fraprie*

New England Road   *Etching by C. W. Anderson*

Crossroads – North Andover, Massachusetts   *Samuel Chamberlain*

Snow and Mist   *Etching by Robert Nisbet*

THE COUNTRYSIDE   93

The Start of the Day *Etching by A. L. Ripley*

Landscape *Etching by C. W. Anderson*

Spring Road – Rochester, New Hampshire   *Samuel Chamberlain*

Snowscape – Beverly, Massachusetts   *Samuel Chamberlain*

THE COUNTRYSIDE

Sugaring-off Time – North Bridgewater, Vermont *Marion Post Wolcott for F.S.A.*

Vermont Valley – near Rutland *Marion Post Wolcott for F.S.A.*

FAIR IS OUR LAND

Skier's Heaven – New Hampshire   *H. E. Adams for U. S. Forest Service*

Winter Hillside – Woodstock, Vermont   *Marion Post Wolcott for F.S.A.*

THE COUNTRYSIDE

Haying Time – Windsor, Vermont   *Rothstein for F.S.A.*

Winter Landscape – Woodstock, Vermont   *Marion Post Wolcott for F.S.A.*

FAIR IS OUR LAND

Road on the Housitanic – New Milford, Connecticut   *Ewing Galloway*

Midsummer – Woodbury, Connecticut   *Samuel Chamberlain*

THE COUNTRYSIDE

Nocturne

Pierson Studio

FAIR IS OUR LAND

Morning After A Snowstorm – Essex, Massachusetts   *Samuel Chamberlain*

Shady Valley   *Etching by R. W. Waiceske*

Windmill – Easthampton, Long Island   *Tet Borsig*

FAIR IS OUR LAND

The Old Swimming Hole – Pine Grove Mills, Pennsylvania *Rosskam for F.S.A.*

Ohio Landscape   *Rothstein for F.S.A.*

Silver Frost in the Adirondacks   *Gustav Anderson*

Thanksgiving Time   *Etching by Peter Marcus*

Minnesota Forest   *Leland J. Prater for U. S. Forest Service*

Footloose – Locust Valley, Long Island *Tet Borsig*

Cherry Blossoms in Washington *Browning*

Early Spring – Tiverton, Rhode Island   *Samuel Chamberlain*

White Face Mountain   *Pierson Studio*

Fruit Blossoms – Aberdeen, Maryland   *Samuel Chamberlain*

Moonshiner's Cabin   *Etching by Chauncey F. Ryder*

Cloud Spots on the Skyline Drive – Virginia   *Samuel Chamberlain*

Silhouette   *Arthur Hammond*

THE COUNTRYSIDE

Greenwood Portico – A Louisiana Plantation   *Frances Benjamin Johnston*

Avenue of Live Oaks – Oak Alley, Louisiana   *Frances Benjamin Johnston*

Early Sugar Mill – Orange City, Florida   *Frances Benjamin Johnston*

The Country Road – South Carolina   *Marion Post Wolcott for F.S.A.*

Church in the Cornfields – Manning, South Carolina *Marion P. Wolcott for F.S.A.*

FAIR IS OUR LAND

Southern Giant *Tet Borsig*

The Swamps *Tet Borsig*

Rappahannock Hills – Virginia   *Rothstein for F.S.A.*

Evergreen Horizon – Virginia   *Rothstein for F.S.A.*

Kentucky Farm Estate   *Marion Post Wolcott for F.S.A.*

Spring Morning – Shenandoah Valley, Virginia   *Marion P. Wolcott for F.S.A.*

THE COUNTRYSIDE

Spring on a Long Island Farm   *Gustav Anderson*

Entrance to Monument Valley   *Cedric Wright*

The Great West

Country Church in Iowa   *Vachon for F.S.A.*

Highway No. 16 – South Dakota   *Ewing Galloway*

FAIR IS OUR LAND

Farm Road in North Dakota   *Vachon for F.S.A.*

Country School – Ward County, North Dakota   *Vachon for F.S.A.*

THE GREAT WEST

The Foothills in Colorado   *Lee for F.S.A.*

The Plains of South Dakota   *Vachon for F.S.A.*

Montana Sheepherder   *Rothstein for F.S.A.*

Colorado Pasture   *Rothstein for F.S.A.*

THE GREAT WEST   121

Cattle Range – Montana   *F. E. Dunham for U. S. Forest Service*

Round-up – Montana   *Rothstein for F.S.A.*

FAIR IS OUR LAND

Sheepherder's Camp   *Paul S. Bieler for U. S. Forest Service*

Sheep Country – Eastern Washington   *Ray Atkeson*

Four Moods of Monument Valley – I. Sunrise   *Josef Muench*

II. Mid-day   *Ernest Knee*

III. Afternoon   *Josef Muench*

IV. Sunset   *Cedric Wright*

THE GREAT WEST

Three Circle Round-up – Montana

Rothstein for F.S.A.

Valley Ranch in Utah

Ray Atkeson

FAIR IS OUR LAND

The Corral – Jackson, Wyoming *Rothstein for F.S.A.*

Desert Bloom *Chuck Abbott*

THE GREAT WEST

Road to the Desert – Utah
Rothstein for F.S.A.

Hopi Village
Chuck Abbott

FAIR IS OUR LAND

Tailings Pit of the Gold Mill – Telluride, Colorado   *Lee for F.S.A.*

Grand Junction Valley – Colorado   *Josef Muench*

Desert Flowers

Esther Henderson

FAIR IS OUR LAND

Hay Stacker – Utah   *Rothstein for F.S.A.*

South Park Colorado in Winter   *Charles B. Abbot*

THE GREAT WEST   131

The Round-up – New Mexico   *W. H. Shaffer for U.S. Forest Service*

Northern New Mexico   *Ernest Knee*

Approaching Storm – Santa Fe, New Mexico   *Ernest Knee*

San Xavier Mission   *Esther Henderson*

Betatakin Cliff Dwellings – Navajo National Monument   *Hubert A. Lowman*

Natural Bridge – Arches National Monument   *Hubert A. Lowman*

FAIR IS OUR LAND

Cliff Dwellers Village – Canyon de Chelly   *Hubert A. Lowman*

The Desert by Day   *Hubert A. Lowman*

Night in the Apache Desert   *Aquatint by Arthur Hall*

FAIR IS OUR LAND

Sand Dunes – Yuma, Arizona   *Hubert A. Lowman*

Indian Houses – Salt River   *Etching by George Elbert Burr*

THE GREAT WEST

"Elephant's Feet" – Near Red Lake, Arizona   *Josef Muench*

Navajo Sheep in Monument Valley   *Chuck Abbott*

Light Snows in Utah   *Lee for F.S.A.*

Fertile Valley – San Cristobal, New Mexico   *Lee for F.S.A.*

THE GREAT WEST

Cactus Country

Chuck Abbott

FAIR IS OUR LAND

Yucca and Wildflowers   *Chuck Abbott*

Desert Nocturne   *Josef Muench*

Bright Angel Point – Grand Canyon

Hubert A. Lowman

FAIR IS OUR LAND

The Grand Canyon *Department of the Interior*

Dead Wood – Grand Canyon *Cedric Wright*

The Bright Angel Trail – Grand Canyon   *Lithograph by Joseph Pennell*

South Rim of the Grand Canyon   *Laura Gilpin*

Early Morning in the Grand Canyon   *Ernest Knee*

THE GREAT WEST

Mitchell Pass – Scotts Bluff National Monument   *Geo. A. Grant for Dept. of the Int.*

Bryce Canyon

Laura Gilpin

FAIR IS OUR LAND

Desert Sycamore   *Esther Henderson*

THE GREAT WEST   147

Santa Anita Pass   *Etching by R. Stephens Wright*

Logging Camp in Oregon   *Lee for F.S.A.*

Elk Hunters   *Etching by Levon West*

Coastal Pastures – California   *Grant Duggins*

THE GREAT WEST   149

Death Valley Dunes   *Geo. A. Grant for U.S. Dept. of the Interior*

Death Valley – California   *Grant Duggins*

Storm on East Escapement – Sierra Nevada   *Cedric Wright*

Grande Ronde Valley – Oregon   *Minor White*

Sky Pastures   *Roi Partridge*

FAIR IS OUR LAND

The Library – University of Virginia   *Samuel Chamberlain*

Our Architectural Inheritance

Springtime in Salem   *Drypoint by Samuel Chamberlain*

Weathered Clapboards   *Samuel Chamberlain*

Church on the Green – Middlebury, Vermont   *Samuel Chamberlain*

The Parson Capen House – Topsfield, Massachusetts   *Samuel Chamberlain*

FAIR IS OUR LAND

Longfellow's Wayside Inn – South Sudbury, Massachusetts   *Samuel Chamberlain*

Bulfinch Hall – Andover, Massachusetts   *Samuel Chamberlain*

Old Buildings in Harvard Yard – Cambridge, Massachusetts   *Samuel Chamberlain*

The State House – Boston, Massachusetts   *Samuel Chamberlain*

FAIR IS OUR LAND

Independence Hall – Philadelphia, Pennsylvania

Ewing Galloway

The Capitol Dome – Washington, D.C.   *Ewing Galloway*

FAIR IS OUR LAND

Mount Vernon   *Frances Benjamin Johnston*

The White House   *Delano for F.S.A.*

OUR ARCHITECTURAL INHERITANCE

The Apothecary's Shop – Williamsburg, Virginia *Drypoint by Samuel Chamberlain*

FAIR IS OUR LAND

Monticello – Near Charlottesville, Virginia   *Samuel Chamberlain*

The Capitol – Williamsburg, Virginia   *Drypoint by Samuel Chamberlain*

OUR ARCHITECTURAL INHERITANCE

Springtime in Williamsburg   *Richard Garrison*

Otwell – Maryland   *Frances Benjamin Johnston*

Sweet Hall – Virginia   *Frances Benjamin Johnston*

Blacklock House – Charleston, South Carolina

Frances Benjamin Johnston

FAIR IS OUR LAND

Church Street – Charleston, South Carolina   *Frances Benjamin Johnston*

Ruins of Sheldon Church – South Carolina   *Frances Benjamin Johnston*

General Bragg's House – Mobile, Alabama   *Frances Benjamin Johnston*

Past Glory – Bellegrove, Louisiana   *Frances Benjamin Johnston*

FAIR IS OUR LAND

Upson House – Athens, Georgia   *Frances Benjamin Johnston*

Belle Helena Plantation – Louisiana   *Vories Fisher*

Greenwood Plantation – Louisiana   *Frances Benjamin Johnston*

The Hermitage – Plantation in Louisiana   *Vories Fisher*

Courtyard in the Vieux Carré – New Orleans   *Frances Benjamin Johnston*

OUR ARCHITECTURAL INHERITANCE

The Old State Capitol – Des Moines, Iowa   *Ewing Galloway*

The Conception Mission – near San Antonio, Texas   *Underwood-Stratton*

Mission San Jose – San Antonio   *Claude B. Aniol*

The Alamo – San Antonio   *Claude B. Aniol*

OUR ARCHITECTURAL INHERITANCE

Tumacacori Mission – Arizona

Hubert A. Lowman

Old Spanish Mission – Taos, New Mexico

Rothstein for F.S.A.

FAIR IS OUR LAND

Mission San Xavier – Arizona *Josef Muench*

Mission San Xavier – Arizona *Esther Henderson*

Far West Architecture – Virginia City, Nevada *Rothstein for F.S.A.*

Old Courthouse – Tombstone, Arizona *Chuck Abbott*

FAIR IS OUR LAND

San Juan Bautista Mission   *Will Connell*

Santa Barbara Mission   *Will Connell*

Santa Ynez Mission   *Grant Duggins*

San Luis Rey Mission   *Grant Duggins*

Yosemite Falls   *Padilla Studios*

Mountain Ranges
and the Nation's Parks

Estes Park – Colorado   *Tet Borsig*

Pike's Peak Beyond A Screen of Saplings   *Laura Gilpin*

Mt. Cannon – Montana　　　　　　　　*Hileman for Glacier National Park*

MOUNTAIN RANGES AND THE NATION'S PARKS

The Mountains in White   *Fritz Kaeser*

The Mountains in Black – West Gate   *Etching by Levon West*

Wintry Silhouette

Josef Muench

MOUNTAIN RANGES AND THE NATION'S PARKS

Goat Mountain – Montana   *Hileman for Glacier National Park*

The Peak   *Etching by Levon West*

FAIR IS OUR LAND

The Mission Range – Montana   *U.S. Forest Service*

The Bad Lands – South Dakota   *Ewing Galloway*

MOUNTAIN RANGES AND THE NATION'S PARKS   185

Wallowa Mountains – Oregon   *Minor White*

Carson Pass – California   *McCurry*

San Francisco Peaks – Arizona

Esther Henderson

MOUNTAIN RANGES AND THE NATION'S PARKS

The Sierras in Midwinter   *Josef Muench*

Mount Shasta   *Ray Atkeson*

Mount Hood   *Ray Atkeson*

Shuksan in Winter   *Etching by Helen A. Loggie*

MOUNTAIN RANGES AND THE NATION'S PARKS   189

Mount Hood   *Ray Atkeson*

The Cascade Range – Washington   *Ray Atkeson*

Trail Approaching Mount Whitney   *Cedric Wright*

Sunset from Muir Pass – California   *Cedric Wright*

Peak of Mount Hood in the Clouds   *Ray Atkeson*

Midwinter on Mount Hood   *Ray Atkeson*

Drift Snow   *Josef Muench*

Reflections in the High Sierra   *Josef Muench*

MOUNTAIN RANGES AND THE NATION'S PARKS

193

Autumn Snow on Mount Adams   *Ray Atkeson*

Alpine Meadows – Mount Rainier   *U.S. Department of the Interior*

Deadwood Drama – Mount Rainier

U.S. Department of the Interior

The Gates of Yosemite Valley   *Ansel Adams for U.S. Department of the Interior*

Yosemite Valley After a Snow Storm   *Ralph Anderson for U.S. Dept. of the Int.*

Sequoias in the Snow   *Ralph Anderson for U.S. Department of the Interior*

El Capitan – Yosemite Valley

U.S. Department of the Interior

FAIR IS OUR LAND

Horse Ridge – Yosemite National Park   *U.S. Department of the Interior*

Half Dome – Yosemite National Park   *Padilla Studios for U.S. Dept. of the Interior*

MOUNTAIN RANGES AND THE NATION'S PARKS

Gunsight Lake   *Hileman for Glacier National Park*

Temple of Tinawana – Zion National Park   *Geo. A. Grant for U.S. Dept. of Interior*

Grinnell Glacier   *Hileman for Glacier National Park*

Glacier Lillies – Mount Clements   *Hileman for Glacier National Park*

MOUNTAIN RANGES AND THE NATION'S PARKS   201

Bear Grass – Mount Gould   *Hileman for U.S. Department of the Interior*

Badger Pass in Winter – Yosemite   *Ansel Adams for U.S. Department of the Interior*

FAIR IS OUR LAND

Mountain Highway

Hileman for Glacier National Park

Blue Pools on Jupiter Terrace – Yellowstone National Park   *Ray Atkeson*

MOUNTAIN RANGES AND THE NATION'S PARKS

The Monarchs – Sequoia National Park   *U.S. Department of the Interior*

Forest Giants   *Gabriel Moulin for U.S. Department of the Interior*

Sunburst   *Ray Atkeson*

Cape Elizabeth – Maine   *Ewing Galloway*

The Seacoasts

Smoke Houses – Thomaston, Maine   *Samuel Chamberlain*

Portland Head Light – Maine   *Ewing Galloway*

FAIR IS OUR LAND

Lobsterman's Cove   *Lithograph by Stow Wengenroth*

After the Rain   *Lithograph by Stow Wengenroth*

THE SEACOASTS

Seine Boats – Gloucester, Massachusetts   *Samuel Chamberlain*

Rocky Neck – Gloucester   *Etching by Max Kuehn*

FAIR IS OUR LAND

The Old Whaler "Charles W. Morgan"   *Samuel Chamberlain*

Boats At Dawn   *Etching by Frank W. Benson*

THE SEACOASTS

The Cliffs of Gay Head – Matha's Vineyard, Massachusetts   *Samuel Chamberlain*

The Gunner's Blind   *Etching by Frank W. Benson*

Race Week – Marblehead, Massachusetts   *Samuel Chamberlain*

Portsmouth Harbor – New Hampshire   *Etching by Charles H. Woodbury*

THE SEACOASTS

Stonington Sunset – Connecticut *Drypoint by Samuel Chamberlain*

Coast Storm *Etching by C. Jac Young*

Coming In   *Etching by C. Jac Young*

"Motif No. 1" – Rockport, Massachusetts   *Gerhard H. Bakker*

THE SEACOASTS

Black Squall

Eleanor Park Custis

FAIR IS OUR LAND

Seine Fishermen   *Eleanor Park Custis*

The Dunes – Montauk Point, Long Island *Tet Borsig*

Net Pattern – Long Island *Tet Borsig*

FAIR IS OUR LAND

Reflections in Boston Harbor

Frank R. Fraprie

THE SEACOASTS

219

The Shore At Montauk Point – Long Island

Tet Borsig

FAIR IS OUR LAND

Oyster Boats – Cape Cod

Ralph E. Day

Lower Manhattan – Seen by the Camera   *Ewing Galloway*

Lower Manhattan – Seen by the Lithographer   *Lithograph by Joseph Pennell*

FAIR IS OUR LAND

The Queen and Her Slaves   *Etching by Otto Kuhler*

Civic Insomnia   *Aquatint by Gerald K. Geerlings*

THE SEACOASTS   223

The Spires of Manhattan   *Etching by Otto Kuhler*

New York Harbor   *Tet Borsig*

Delaware Fishing Village   *Vachon for F.S.A.*

Oyster Boats in Deal's Island Bay   *Delano for F.S.A.*

THE SEACOASTS

Shores of Maryland   *Soft Ground Etching by F. Townsend Morgan*

Fishing Fleet – Hampton, Virginia   *Samuel Chamberlain*

FAIR IS OUR LAND

Windswept   *Etching by Alfred Hutty*

Sand Dunes – St. Augustine, Florida *Arthur Hammond*

Beach Grass – Florida *Arthur Hammond*

The Breakers   *Ray Atkeson*

THE SEACOASTS   229

Wings Against The Sky – Mississippi *Anthony V. Ragusin*

The Oyster Fleet – Biloxi, Mississippi *Anthony V. Ragusin*

FAIR IS OUR LAND

Florida Shore   *Arthur Hammond*

Pacific Sands   *Brett Weston*

California Surf   *Robert Ingram*

FAIR IS OUR LAND

Fish Harbor   *Etching by R. Stephens Wright*

Snug Harbor   *Etching by Armin Hanson*

Small Mission Wharf   *Etching by John W. Winkler*

View from Telegraph Hill – San Francisco   *Etching by John W. Winkler*

Fishermen's Wharf – San Francisco   *Robert Ingram*

THE SEACOASTS   235

Puget Sound – Washington

Etching by R. Stephens Wright

Venice in Oakland

Roi Partridge

FAIR IS OUR LAND

Compositon at Low Tide

Roi Partridge

Arch Cape – Oregon

Ray Atkeson

FAIR IS OUR LAND

Cape Kiwanda – Oregon   *Ray Atkeson*

Cannon Beach – Oregon   *Ray Atkeson*

THE SEACOASTS

The Pacific   *Roi Partridge*

STONE BARN   *Wood Engraving by Thomas W. Nason*

List of Illustrations

FAIR IS OUR LAND

THE FARM

LIST OF ILLUSTRATIONS

MOUNTAIN RANGES AND THE NATION'S PARKS